Feng Shaun

Discover Inner Peace with Shaun the Sheep

Simon & Schuster
Rockefeller Center
1230 Avenue of the Americas
New York, NY 10020

Text copyright © 2002 by Macmillan Publishers Ltd.

Originally published in Great Britain in 2002 by Boxtree,
an imprint of Pan Macmillan Ltd.

SIMON & SCHUSTER and colophon are registered trademarks
of Simon & Schuster, Inc.

For information regarding special discounts for bulk purchases,
please contact Simon & Schuster Special Sales at 1-800-456-6798
or business@simonandschuster.com

Designed by Dan Newman, Perfect Bound

Manufactured in Belgium

3 5 7 9 10 8 6 4

Produced under license by Aardman Animations ©
and ™ Aardman/Wallace and Gromit Ltd. 2002

ISBN 0-7432-5410-4

Feng Shaun

Discover Inner Peace with Shaun the Sheep

Simon & Schuster

New York   London   Toronto   Sydney   Singapore

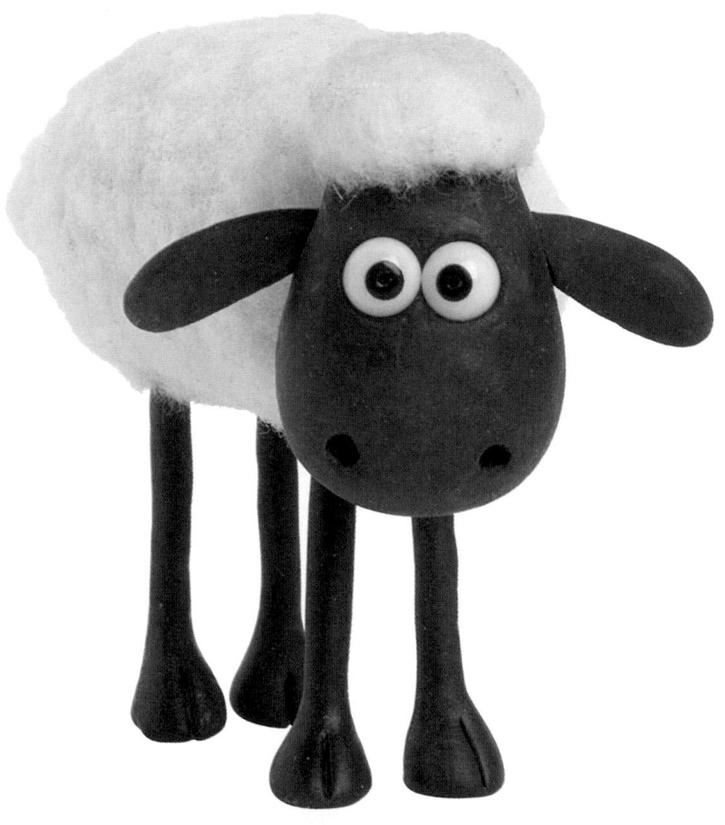

*Wear white, natural fabrics
to induce a feeling of calm
and purity*

Clutter blocks vital energy, leading to frustration and subtle obstacles in your life

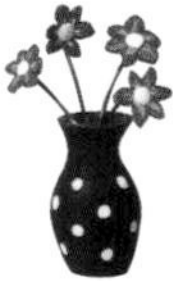

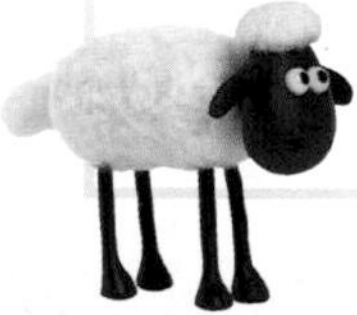

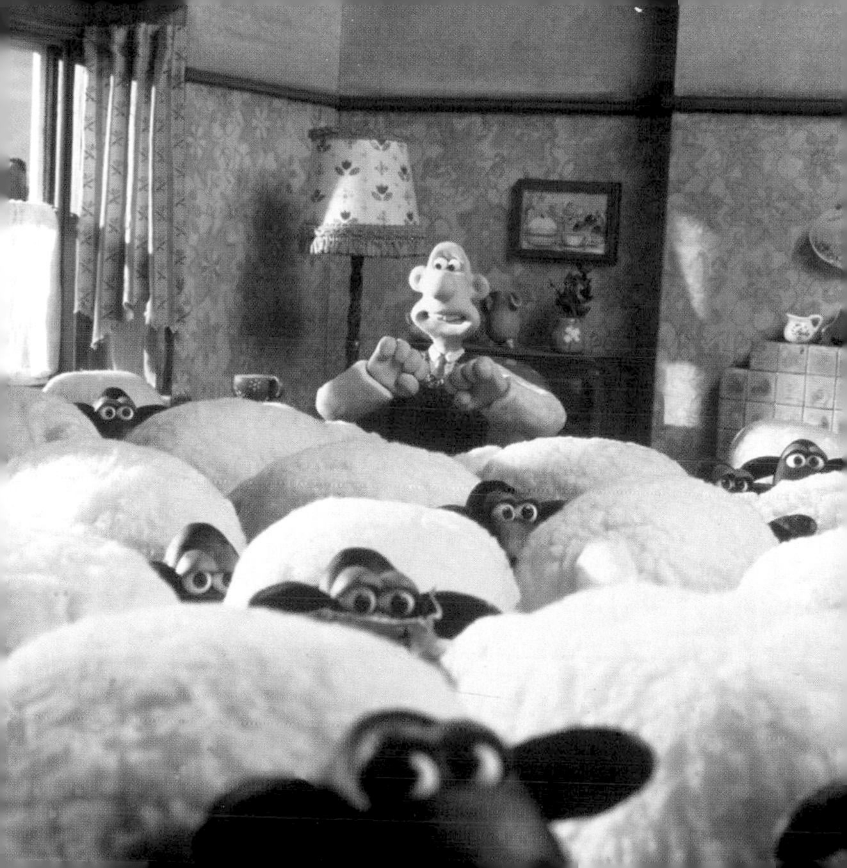

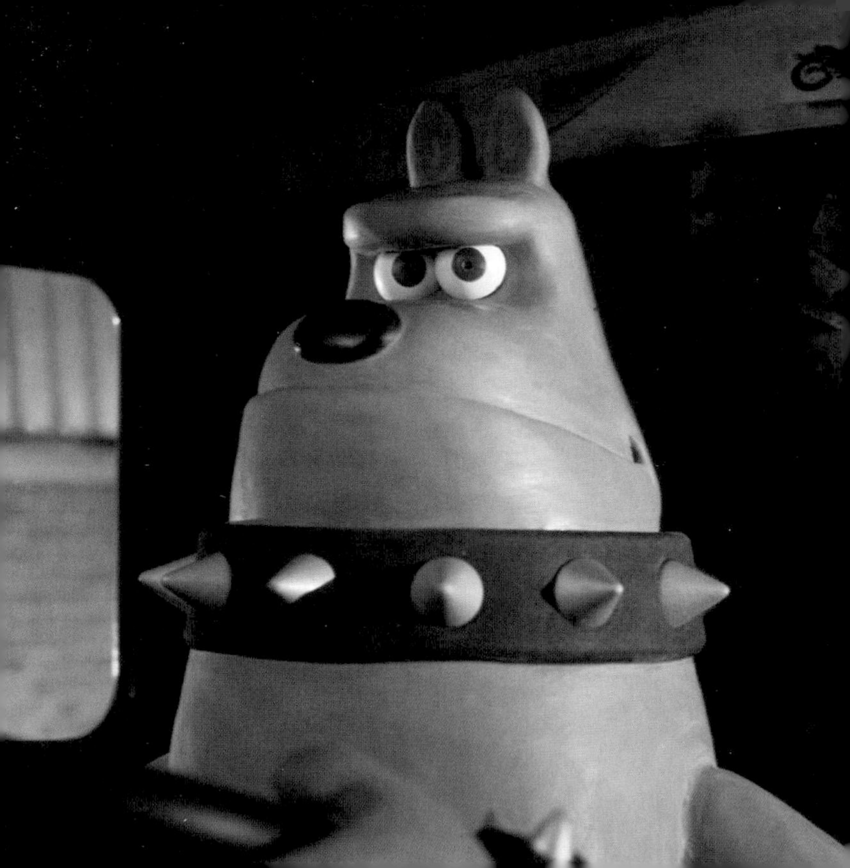

CULTIVATE YOUR SOUL

Spending more time in good company and less time in bad company will have a positive effect on your mental and spiritual wellbeing

TAKE YOUR MIND OFF THINGS

Slow, repetitive tasks are a great way to ease an anxious mind

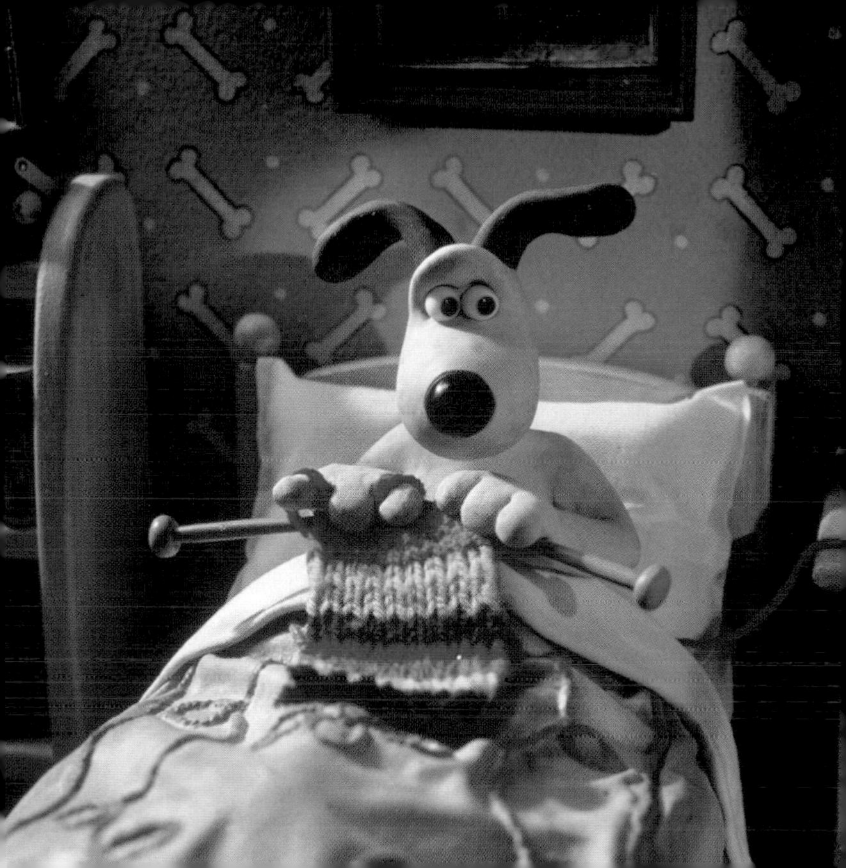

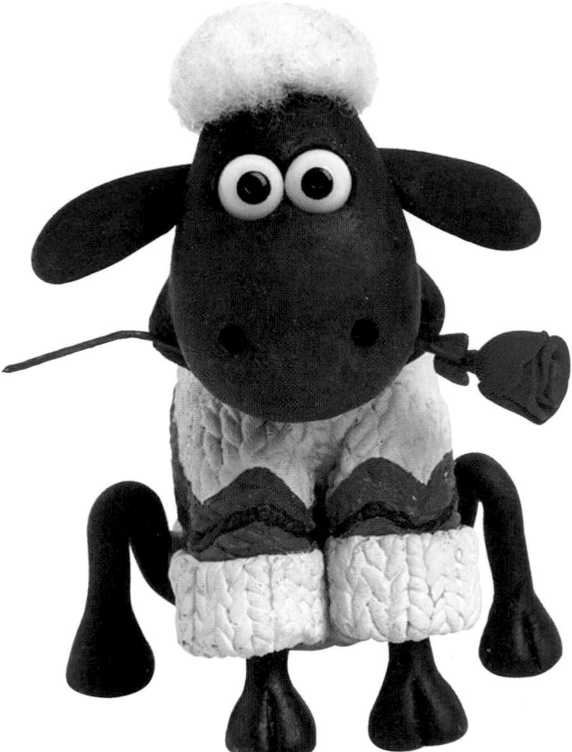

LOVE—MAKING

Introduce love into your life – it has a positive affect on your thinking patterns and endorphin levels

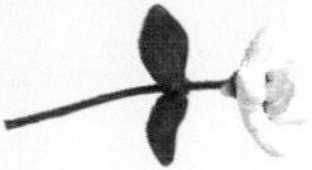

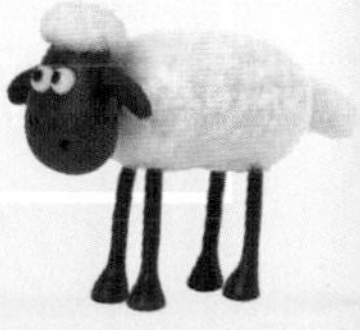

HAVE FAITH

*Prayer is often the only
solution to certain
insurmountable problems*

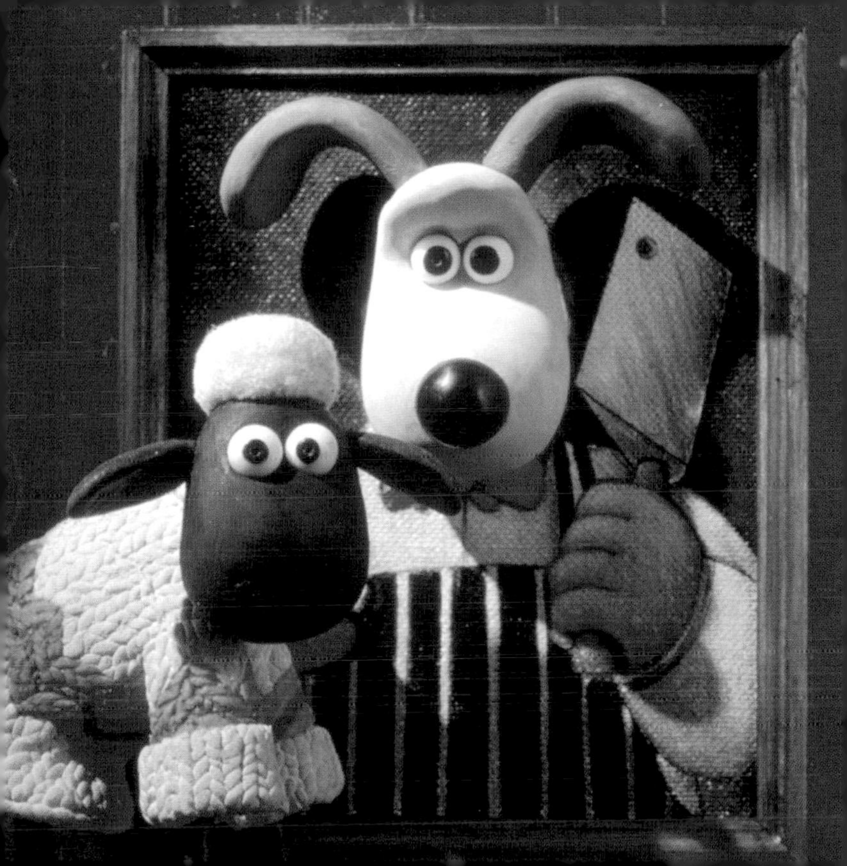

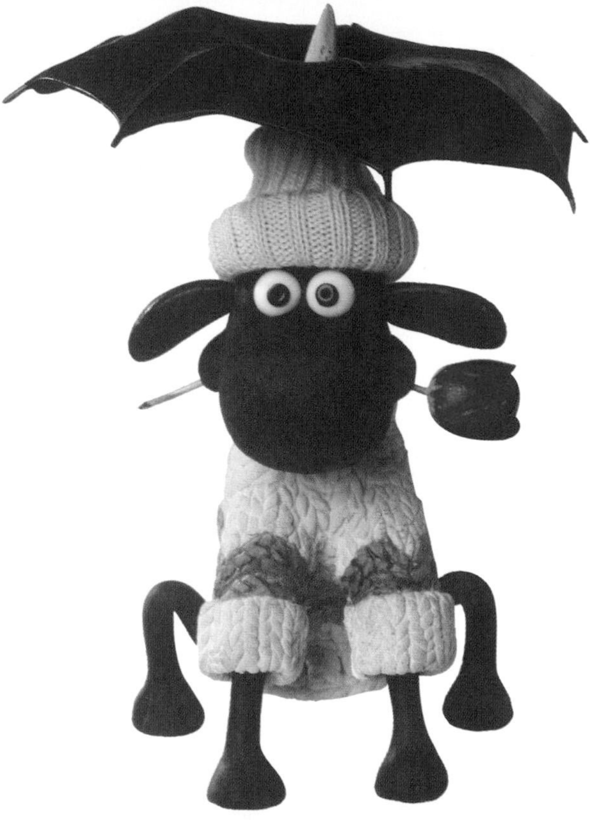

LOOK GOOD, FEEL GREAT!

Personal grooming is essential for increasing self-esteem. Make sure you look your very best every day

Understand your cravings and addictions – they show a lack of control and cause unhappiness

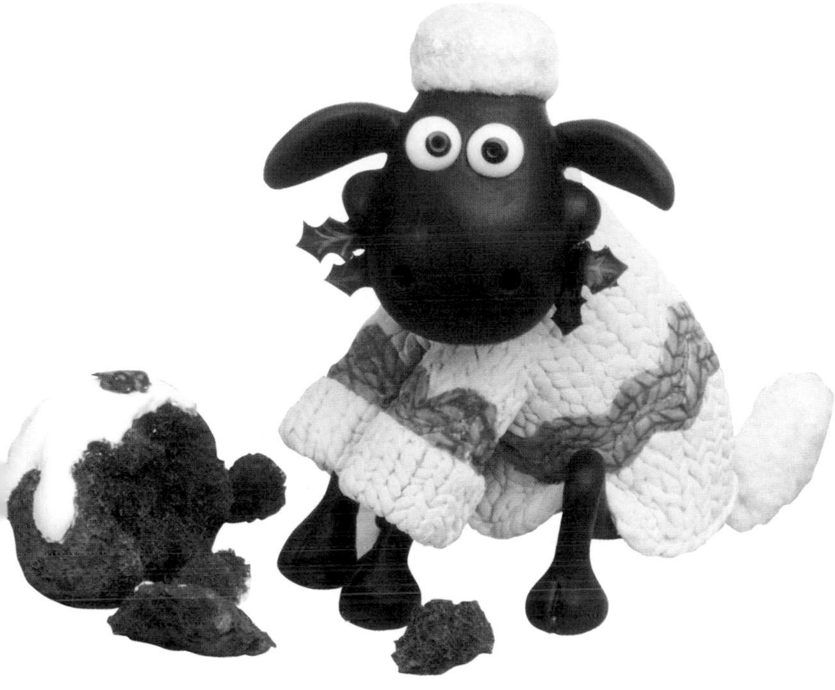

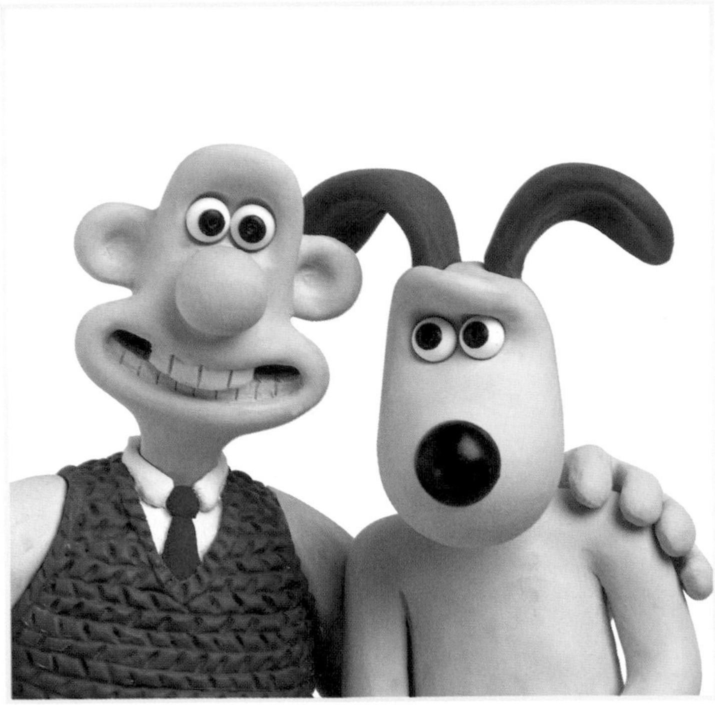

One of the surest ways of soothing anxiety is through touch. An arm on a shoulder is a simple gesture that can sometimes work wonders

*Even basic Tai Chi
can lead to instant
feelings of calm*

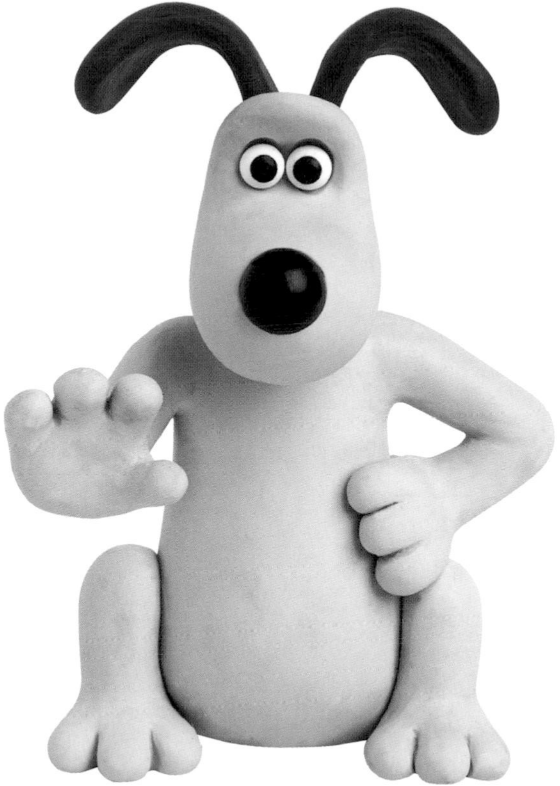

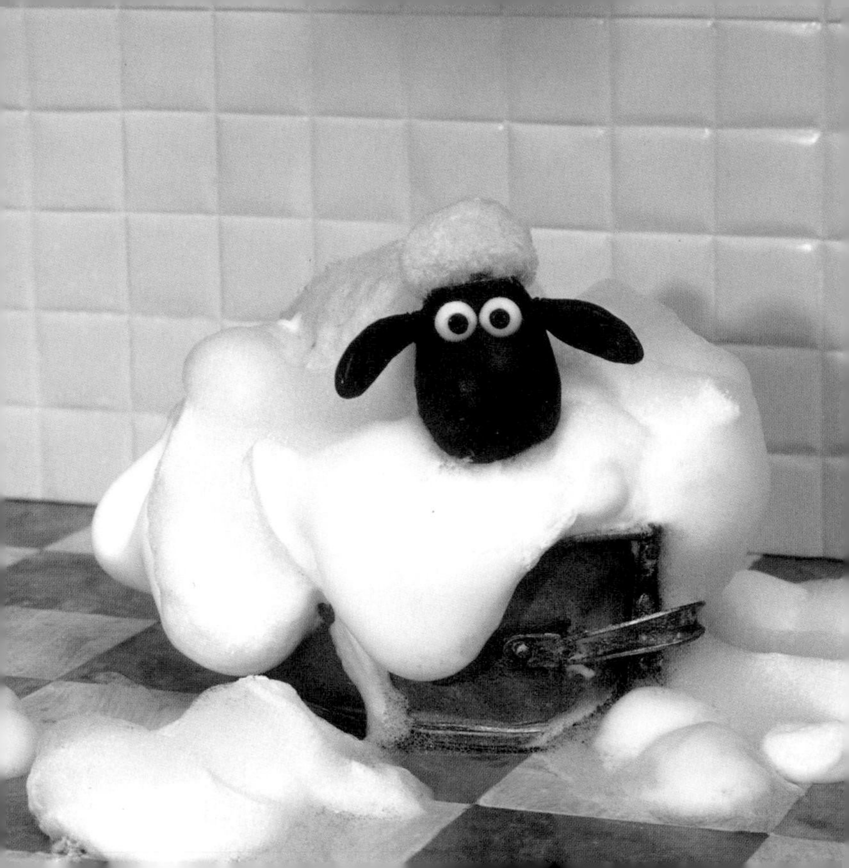

BUBBLES AND TROUBLES

After a hard day, there's nothing better than a good long soak to revive and refresh that tired old body

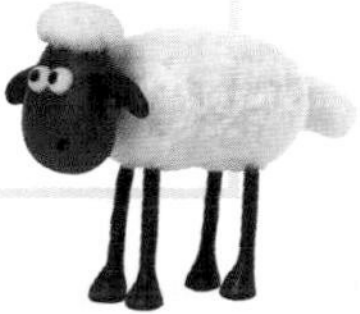

Remember to take every opportunity to inject some passion into your relationship. It will do wonders for body and soul

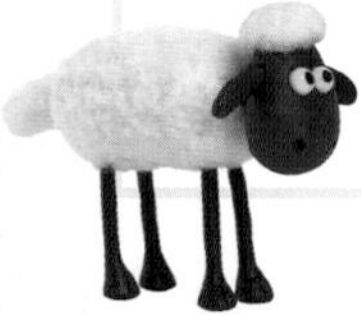

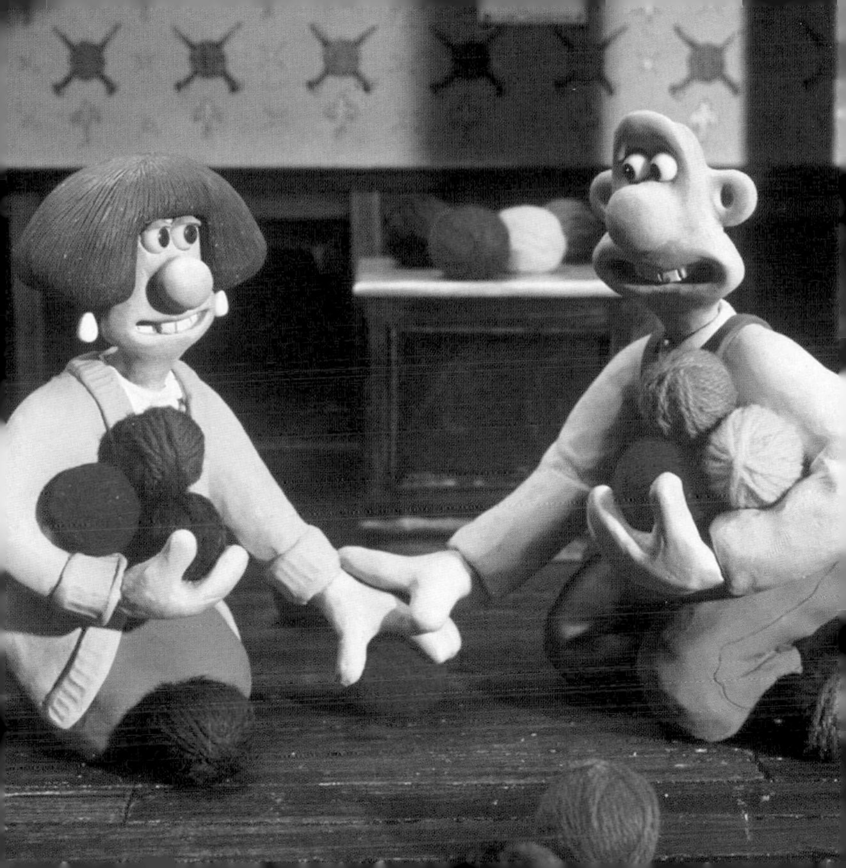

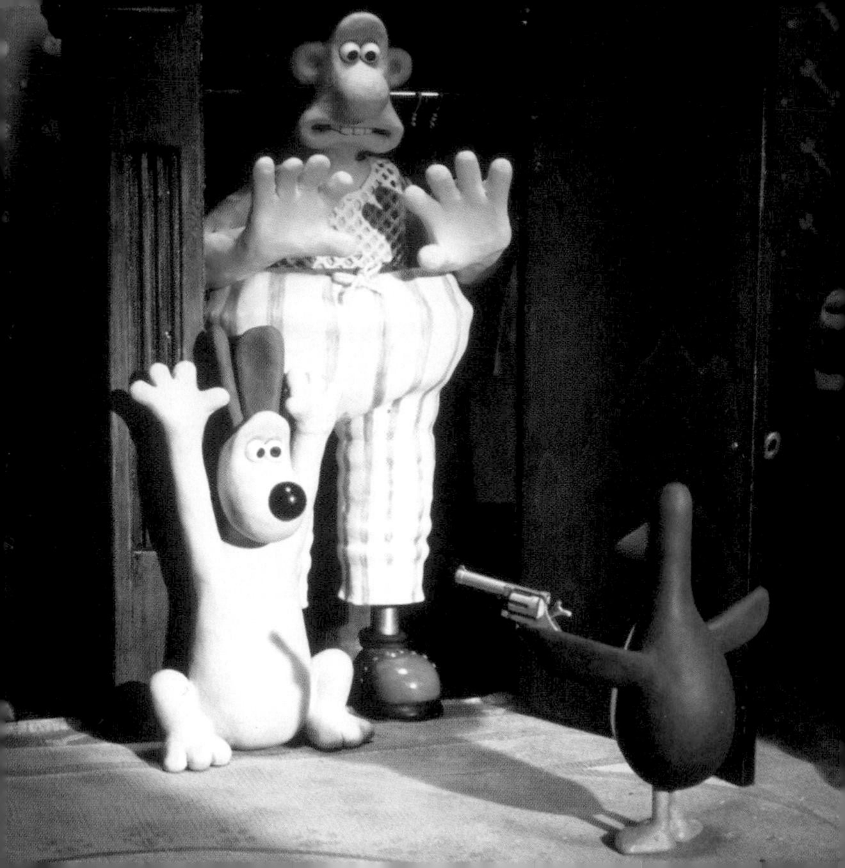

UNDER PRESSURE

Try not to over-react
in times of stress

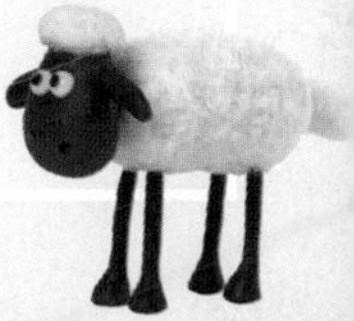

*If in doubt, run away
from trouble. Exercise is a great
way of alleviating tension*

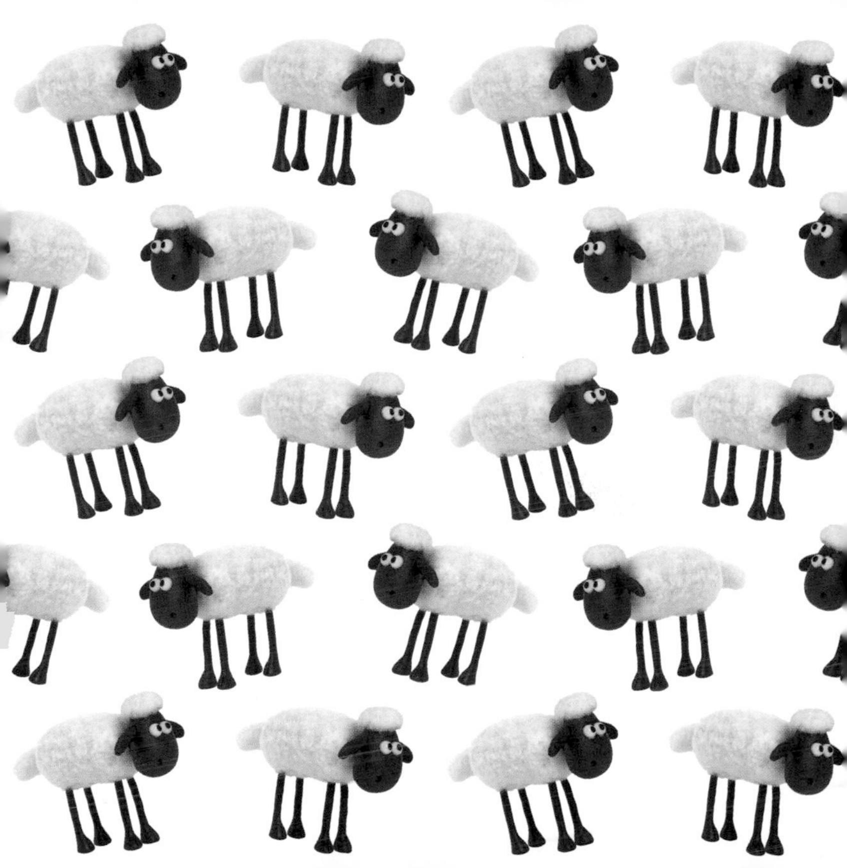

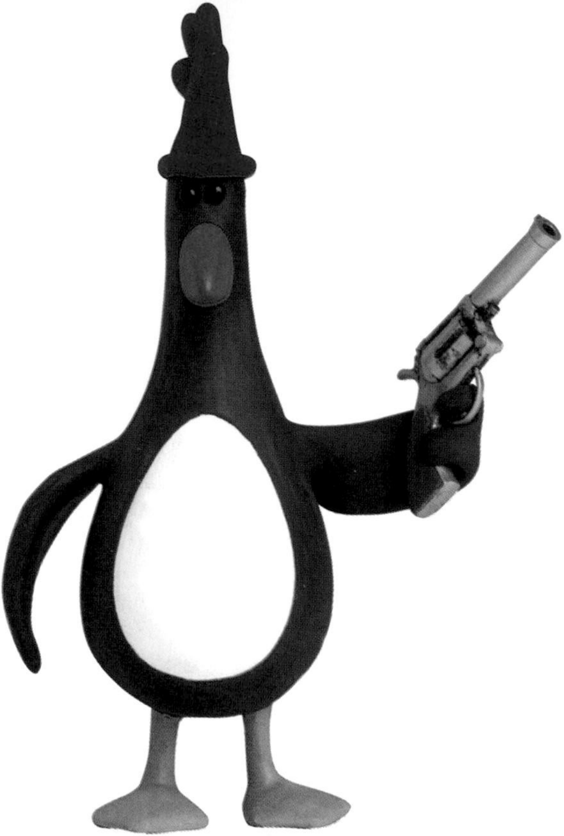

JUST LEAVE ME ALONE!

*There comes a time when
you need to protect and
barricade yourself from
potentially stressful situations*

IRRITABLE BOWEL?

If you're feeling bloated and gassy, watch your diet. A sore tummy is often due to rich and fatty foods

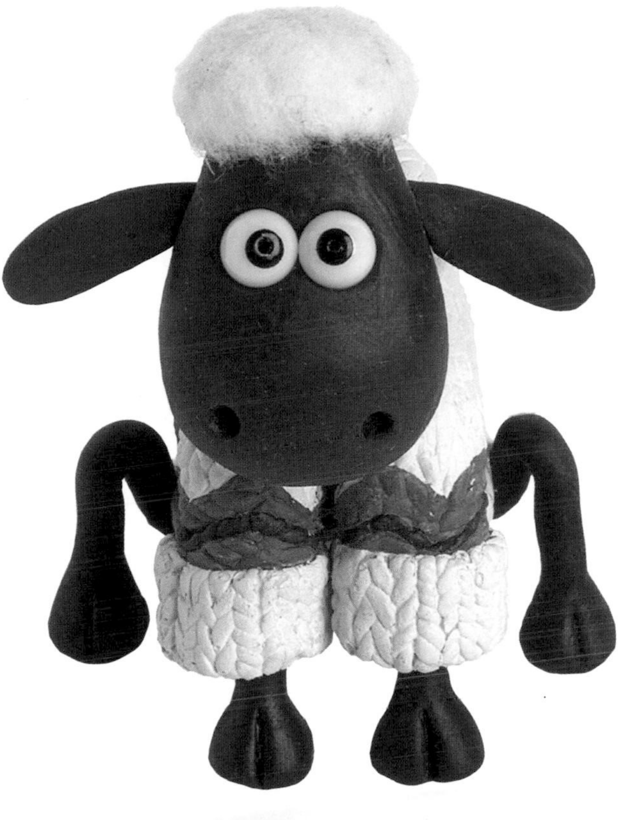

BE OPEN–MINDED

Make friends with new people. Look beyond appearances and remember, strangers are just friends we haven't met

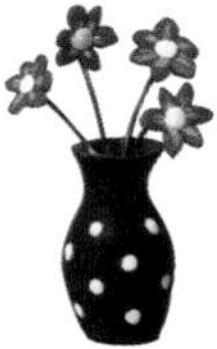

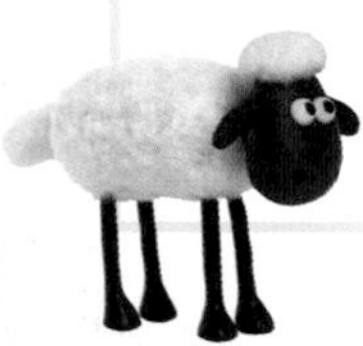

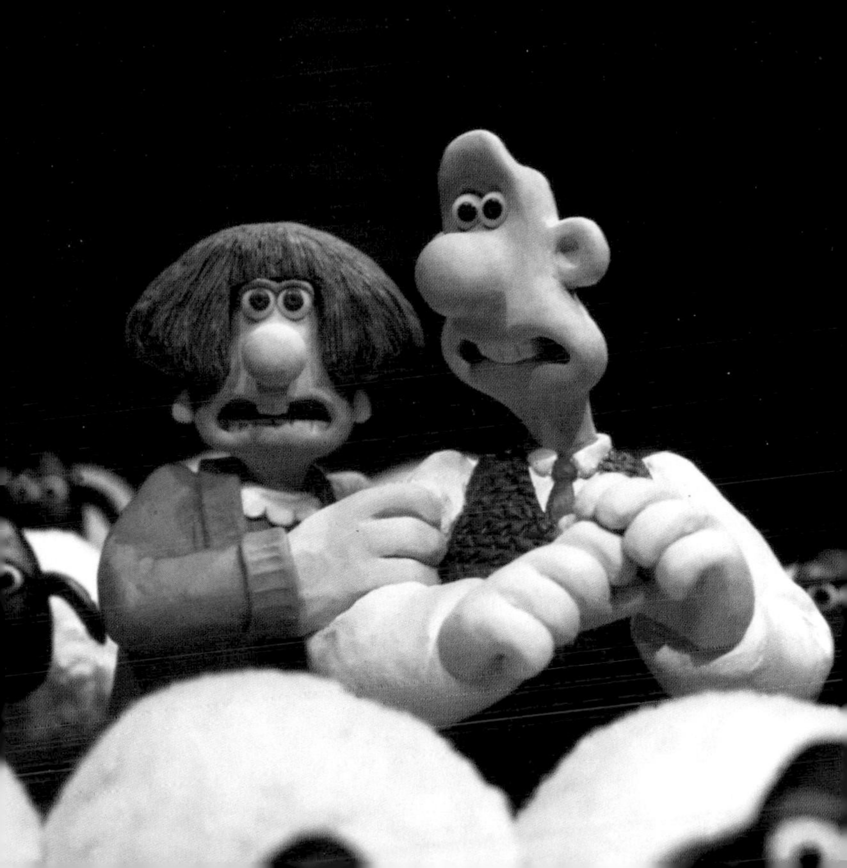

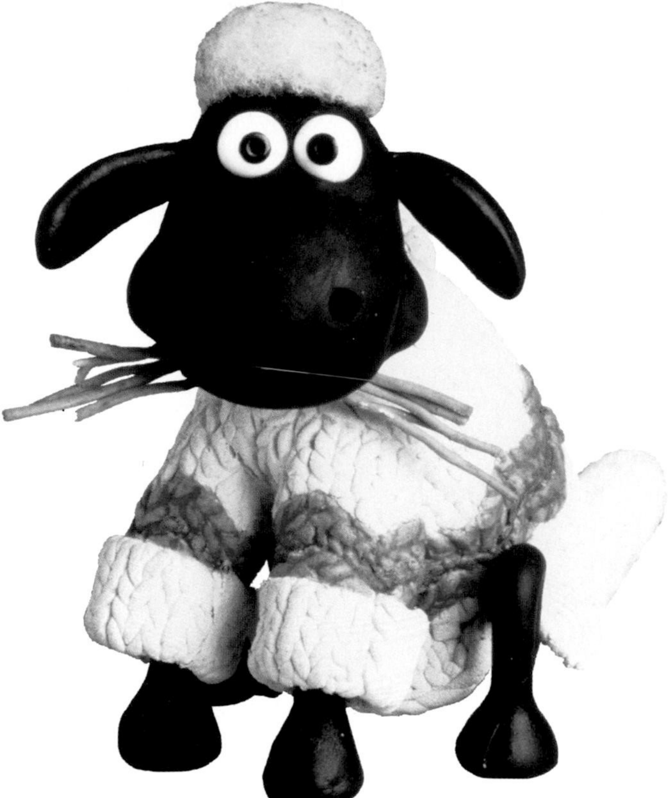

*Eat more greenery – it's the perfect
snack food for body and soul*

Dealing with anxiety in a calm, dignified manner nourishes your inner self

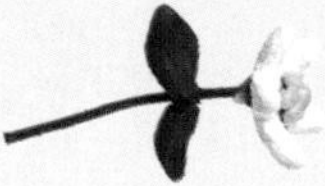

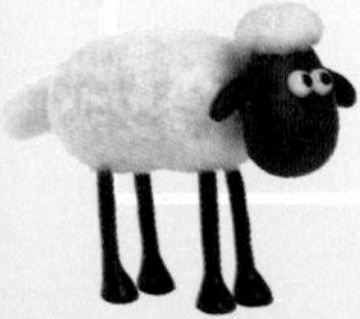

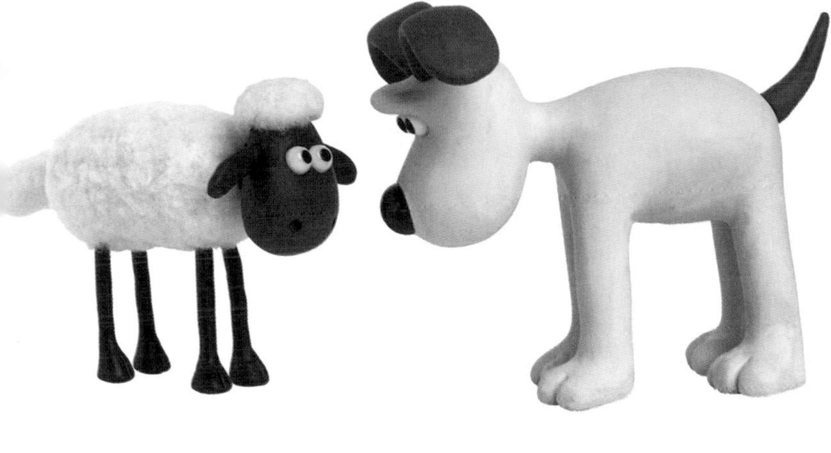

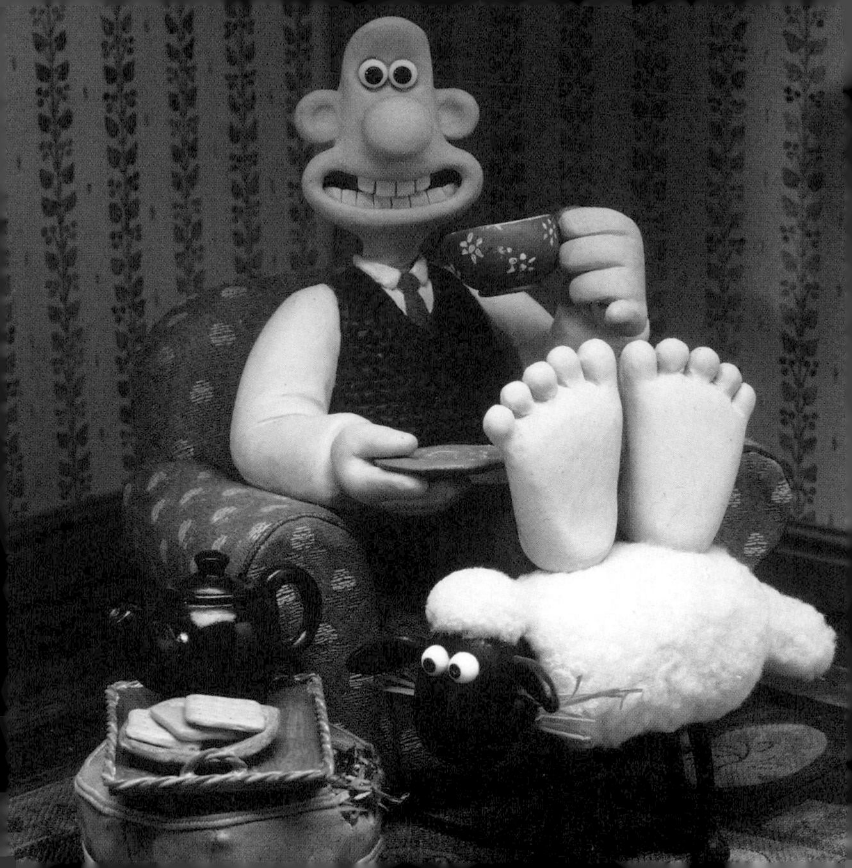

LIMIT YOUR CAFFEINE INTAKE

Between four and six cups of coffee or tea a day and you are over your caffeine limit. Too much caffeine can make you hyperactive

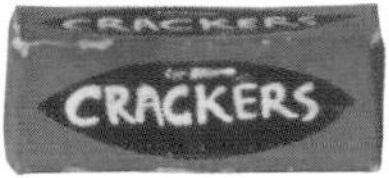
CRACKERS

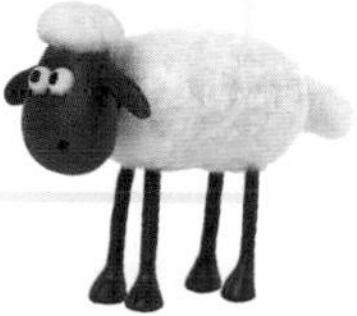

TO ERR IS HUMAN, TO FORGIVE DIVINE

Anger is a negative emotion – be bigger than your enemies and forgive others as often as you can

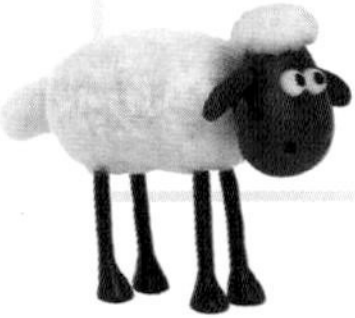

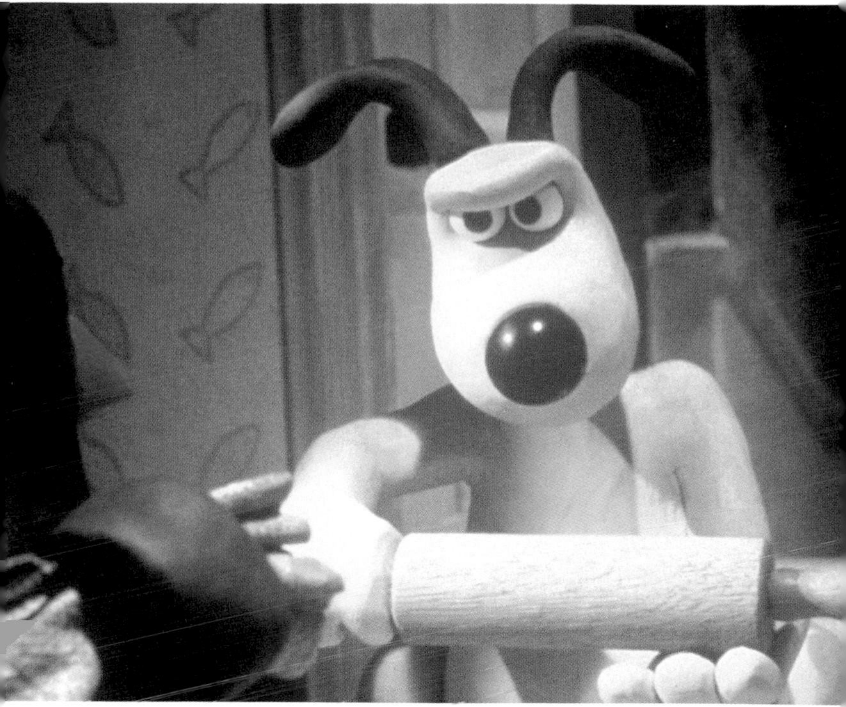

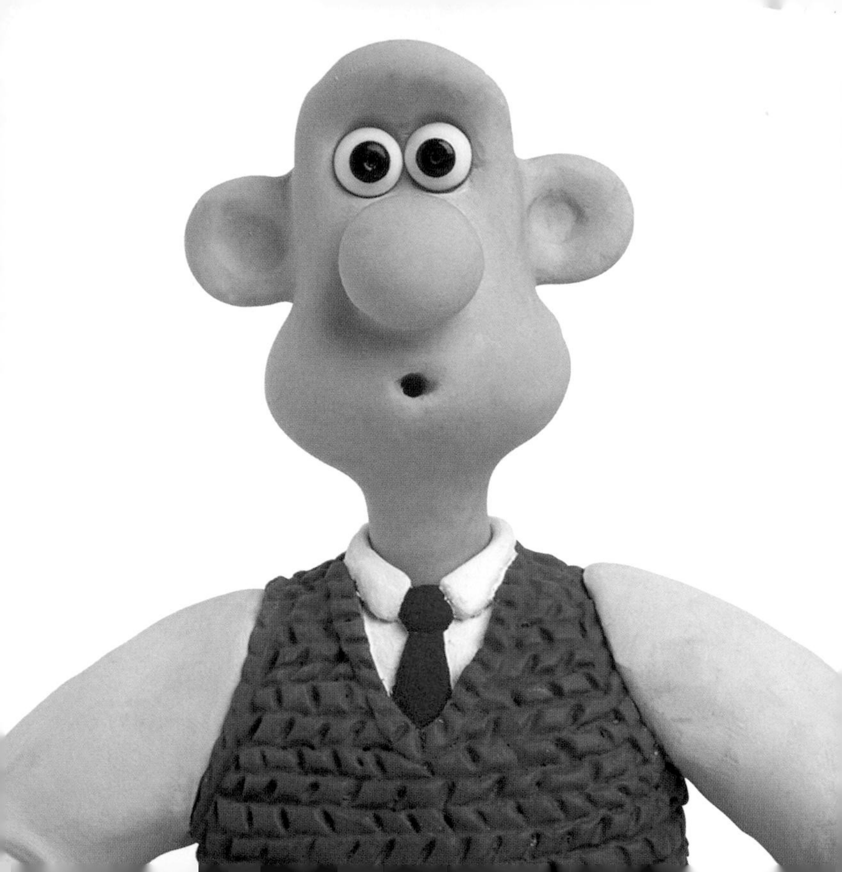

BREATHE DEEPLY

When feeling pressured, breathe
in slowly through the nose
and out through the mouth.
You will soon begin to feel relaxed

AND FINALLY . . .

Read this book as often as you can – on the bus, on the tube or train, in a quiet field . . . whenever you feel your blood starting to boil, your stress levels rising and your hands forming a fist.

Remember your pal Shaun is there for you – don't forget the simple tenets of his wisdom and . . .

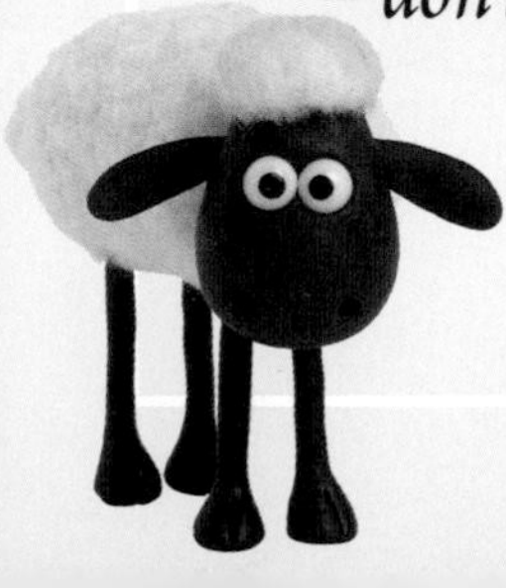

JUST TAKE IT EASY!